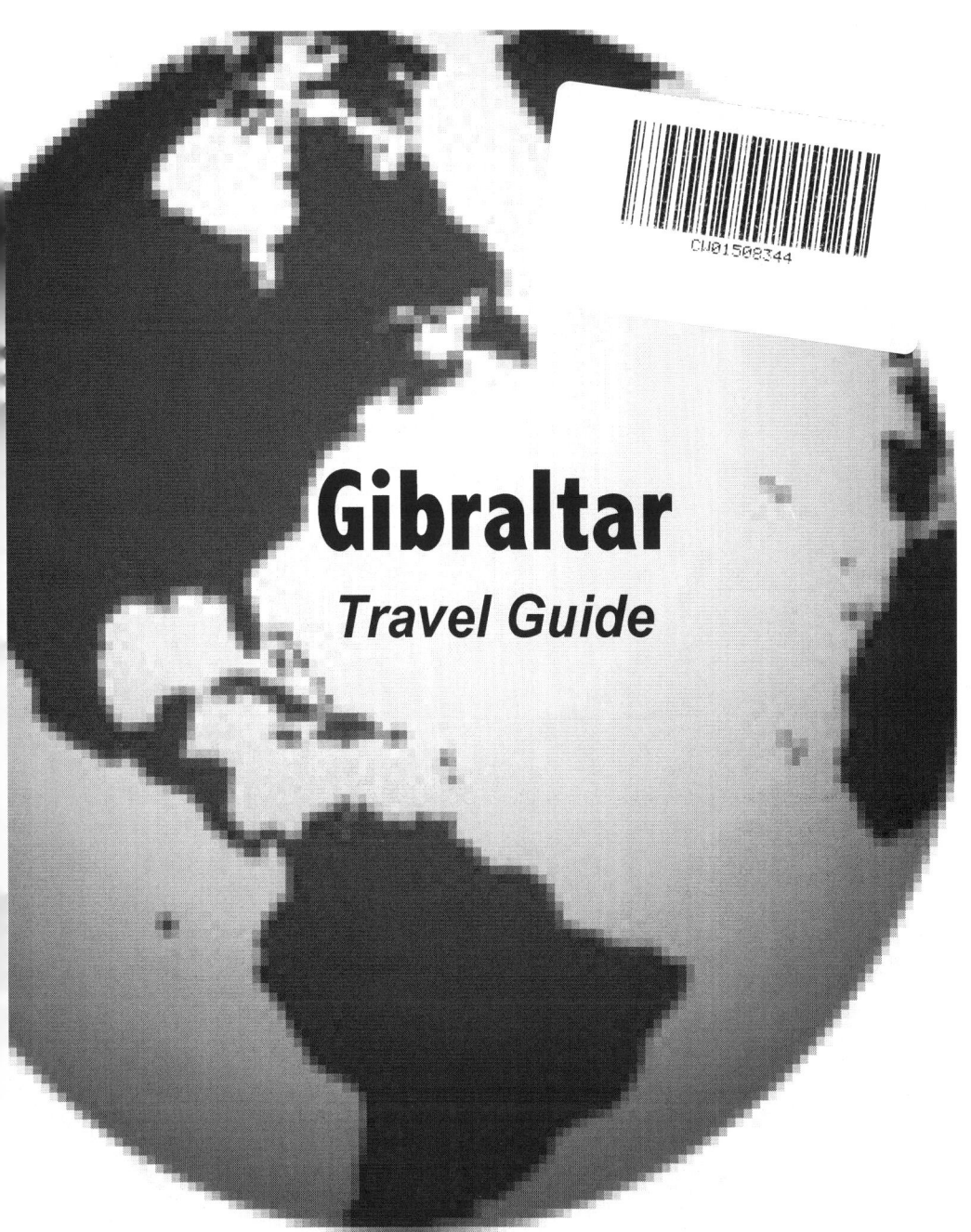

Gibraltar

Travel Guide

Quick Trips Series

Table of Contents

Gibraltar

The Rock of Gibraltar is a beautiful outcrop close to

Spain's Costa del Sol. For more than two centuries it has

been a possession of the United Kingdom. Gibraltar's

interesting caves and labyrinthine tunnels fascinate its visitors.

Neanderthal remains provide proof of early hominid settlement, but from the 700s, Gibraltar fell under Moorish rule. With the Reconquesta, the outpost, which had always carried enormous strategic significance, reverted to Spanish rule.

In 1704, the island's fate took an unusual twist when the Anglo-Dutch forces of George Rooke captured the town and a decade later the Treaty of Utrecht ceded its control to the Crown of Great Britain. Spain failed to reclaim this remote portion of the land either by warfare or politics. As recently as 2002, the people of Gibraltar voted overwhelmingly to maintain the status quo of British rule.

GIBRALTAR TRAVEL GUIDE

As a military outpost of some importance, Gibraltar had been besieged fourteen times in its exciting history and any military buff would be particularly tickled to explore the island, as many of its facilities had military origins or functions. During World War Two, Gibraltar provided the Allied Forces with an excellent base from which to control all sea traffic entering the Mediterranean Sea from the west, and also from which to launch Operation Torch, the campaign to capture the French territories in North African. One interesting fact is that Gibraltar has more tunnels than roads.

Equally compelling is its wildlife. The Rock of Gibraltar is home to the only primate species to occur on the European continent - Barbary Macaques. As these large apes can also be found in the Atlas Mountains of North Africa, it could be speculated that they arrived here with the Moors. An alternate theory suggests the possibility that they were once prolific across much of Europe, but had grown extinct everywhere but here. A persistent legend states that as long as the Barbary Macaques endure, so will the British rule of Gibraltar.

Gibraltar offers a variety of seasonal delights. It is located along the migratory flight path of several species of birds and also attracts a splendid variety of butterflies in the spring time. Dolphins use the shelter of the Strait as a nursery, making the Rock a great base for dolphin watching expeditions. Gibraltar has several beaches, of which the largest is Eastern Bay. The beaches on the western side of Gibraltar tend to be more rocky, but these are popular for jet-skiing and swimming.

The name Gibraltar originated with the conquest of the territory, originally known as Mons Calpe, by a Berber chief by the name of Tarik Ibn Zeyad. He renamed the area Jebel Tarik or Tarik's Rock and the moniker stuck through the ages to come.

Among the famous people who have celebrated their happy nuptials on the Rock are John Lennon and Yoko Ono, as well as two James Bonds - Sean Connery and Roger Moore.

Customs & Culture

The typical native of Gibraltar is a blend of Maltese, Genoan, Portuguese and Spanish blood, but the Indian, British and Moroccan nations are also well represented. Although English is the official language, many residents speak Spanish as well.

There are three main periods of occupation in the history of Gibraltar. The Moors held the Rock for the longest and although the Spanish tried to erase much of the Muslim legacy, a certain North African influence does linger. Geographically, Spain's proximity also impacts on Gibraltar. It came to be a British possession during the 18th Century Regency period and remains so to this day.

Most of the Rock's permanent residents are fluent in both English and Spanish. For a small territory, Gibraltar displays a remarkable religious diversity, accommodating Hindus and Jews alongside Catholics, Anglicans and members of the Church of Scotland. The vast majority of the inhabitants are Roman Catholic. Typical cuisine of Gibraltar includes a blend of English, Spanish, French, Italian and North African.

🌐 Geography

Only 14.3 km separate Africa from Europe across the Strait of Gibraltar. It is located on a peninsula at the southwestern edge of Spain, but falls under the administration of Britain. It guards entry from the west into the Mediterranean Sea.

GIBRALTAR TRAVEL GUIDE

Gibraltar covers fairly modest proportions - 5km long and no more than 1.2km wide - and it is perfectly possible to get around most of the Rock on foot, as long as you don't mind a long walk uphill! There is a bus service with its central terminus located at Casemates Square. If you do organize your own vehicle, be advised that parking is limited and there is usually a daunting traffic bottleneck at Gibraltar's exit points to Spain.

🌐 Weather & Best Time to Visit

The warmest months on Gibraltar are the months of July and August, when average maximum temperatures can be expected of around 27 degrees Celsius and higher. June and September are still fairly warm and even in May and October the mercury touches 20 degrees Celsius.

GIBRALTAR TRAVEL GUIDE

Although the months between June and September see little rainfall, the atmosphere can be somewhat humid.

The wettest months on the other hand, are November, December and March, with January, February and April still seeing a smattering of downpour. The Alameda Botanical Gardens records an annual rainfall of 768mm.

The winter average temperatures hover around 15 degrees Celsius, rising to 17 degrees Celsius in April and November. The weather is, however, mostly sunny year round. The area experiences periodic incoming breezes from the North of Africa.

Sights & Activities: What to See & Do

Upper Rock Nature Reserve

The most convenient way to reach the Nature Reserve as

well as the apes is by the cable car, which can be found

on the southern end of Main Street, right next door to the

Alameda Botanical Gardens. The trip to the top lasts 6

minutes. At the top, there is also a restaurant and

restroom and you can enjoy a panoramic view, which includes Marbella on Costa del Sol, the port of Algeciras in Spain and Morocco. At the Top Station, you will also find Calpe Suite, where weddings may be conducted.

A more adventurous way of reaching the Upper Rock is by the Mediterranean Steps. Although still somewhat challenging, the Mediterranean Steps have recently been upgraded to make them safer for hikers. In springtime, the route proliferates with flowers and the sun is more tolerable. One species to look out for is the rare Gibraltar Campion flower or Silenetomentosa, to use its scientific name, but Gibraltar is home to a wide variety of plant species, many of them related to the vegetation of North Africa, but adapted to Gibraltar's unique combination of limestone and sandstone.

If you fear the climb might be too much of a strain, you could consider using the steps for your descent, as the view is quite spectacular in places. The route was created by the military to connect Jews Gate with the batteries at the summit of the rock.

The mostly unspoilt plant and animal life of the Upper Rock Nature Reserve is one of the highlights on the itinerary of any visitor to Gibraltar. Over 300 species of birds live here. These include the heron, the egret, the ibis, the white stork, the spoonbill and several types of vultures, hawks, harriers, buzzards and eagles. There are also rabbits, mice, red foxes and mouse-eared bats on Gibraltar. Another of its rarer inhabitants is the Mediterranean Monk Seal, which is close to extinct.

🌍 The Gibraltar Apes

The most popular animal species is without a doubt the Barbary macaques.

Although there had been various theories regarding their origin, DNA analysis has confirmed beyond doubt that the Gibraltar Barbary macaques originated in North Africa. One theory suggests that they may have come via the deeper sections of St Michael's cave. They are classed as apes rather than monkeys since they are tailless.

There are several locations about the reserve where you can expect to encounter large colonies of the apes. One troupe roams in close proximity to the upper cable station, while another tend to frequent Apes Den, which is located near the middle station. From April to September, the cable car does not stop here, but it is possible to walk down via the Phillip II steps along the way from St Michael's Cave.

A well-known legend proclaims that British rule of Gibraltar is closely tied with the fate of the Barbary macaques on the Rock. Should the apes ever die out - a scenario that seemed a possibility during World War Two when only seven of the original colony remained - the days of British occupation would also be numbered. Fortunately the ape population numbers almost 300 these days.

While the apes are used to a human presence, you should always remember that they are still creatures of the wild and can display unpredictable behaviour, if they feel threatened. They can be very entertaining and playful, especially when there are juveniles about. Do remember, it is illegal to feed the apes. Disregarding this directive carries a penalty of £500 and since they are quite familiar with human trappings, they are perfectly capable of snatching treats such as ice cream from an unsuspecting tourist and landing him or her in trouble. To be on the safe side, do not touch them, eat in their vicinity or carry bagsthat might be construed as containing food.

🌍 The Tunnels

Midway up at the northern end of the rock, Gibraltar

The Siege Tunnels at Gibraltar can be accessed via the Nature Reserve. They date back to a defensive strategy employed during the Great Siege of 1779 to 1783. In 1782, matters seemed dire. The Spanish were closing and none of the existing batteries were in position to initiate fire on them. The governor of the time, General Elliot offered a reward to anyone who could conceive a plan to position a cannon on the North Face of Gibraltar and the Siege Tunnels, a solution offered by Sergeant-Major Ince, were the result. The holes cut into the limestone to improve ventilation, can still be seen today.

The Siege Tunnels were extended upon during World War Two. By moving water supplies, power generators and medical facilities underground, Britain minimized at least some of the potential damage from hostile fire. During this period, a length of about 48 km was added to the tunnels.

Today, the tunnels are a museum, which displays various aspects of their creation, as well was what it was like for contemporary soldiers to spend extended periods of time inside. The sheer magnitude of digging the extensive network with relatively primitive tools awes most visitors.

Although Gibraltar's underground facilities still fall under the jurisdiction of the Ministry of Defence, the public can view sections of it. A guided tour of the World War Two tunnels, with Hay's Level as starting point, can be arranged.

🌐 Europa Point

One must-see stop on the itinerary of any visitor to Gibraltar is Europa Point, the southernmost part of Gibraltar. From the lookout point, you will be able to see the Atlas Mountains on the other side of the Strait. It is widely believed that these two points had been known as the Pillars of Hercules in ancient times. In fact, Greek myth suggests that mighty Hercules created the Strait of Gibraltar to fulfil one of his legendary tasks.

Three main buildings occupy the site. The Mosque Ibrahim al Ibrahim, the most recent of the three, dates back to 1997. Ironically, the Shrine of Our Lady of Europa had been the mosque in olden times, before the Spaniards converted it to a Catholic emblem. Records from the time indicate that this place of devotion may have provided illumination in earlier times, but the current lighthouse at Gibraltar dates back to 1838. It is still functional. An all-day bus ticket to Europa Point costs

£1.50. Do bear in mind that this location can get quite windy.

Lighthouse at Europa Point

The lighthouse at Europa Point was constructed between 1838 and 1842. Until the time of its completion, Our Lady of Europa had served as beacon and guiding light. Located 50m above sea level, illumination from the lighthouse is visible from a distance of up to 27km. It was a vast improvement, but over time, more upgrades came.

In 1894, the lantern was expanded from a single wick to eight wicks and in 1905, the oil burner was replaced by incandescent light. A foghorn was added, and in 1956, the lighting was further modernized. The tower was increased by 1.83 m and a fixed red light was installed. Its giant

3000-watt bulb can be seen up to 33km away on a clear night. The lighthouse became fully automated in 1994 and is still in use today.

Our Lady of Europe

Serene and seated on her opulent throne, she oversees all that passes the Strait of Gibraltar. According to tradition, seafarers would sometimes come ashore to present

special devotional gifts to the Lady. Among those who have honored this custom were Don Juan de Austria, commander of the Spanish naval forces at the Battle of Lepanto and Giovanni Andrea Doria of Genoa. The marble of her altar was a Papal gift and in May 2009, a Golden Rose was presented to the Bishop of Gibraltar by

Pope Benedict XVI to commemorate the 700th anniversary of the shrine of Our Lady of Europe.

The current statue is not the original one. The Spanish King had installed a limestone monument in 1309, when the Spanish first took possession of Gibraltar, but when the Muslims recaptured the Rock in 1333, the Christians fled, taking Our Lady of Europa with them. By the time Henry IV once again conquered Gibraltar for the Christian Spanish forces in 1462, the whereabouts of the original statue were unknown.

A new statue was commissioned, but an attack by the Turkish pirates of Barbarossa in 1540, mutilated the statue. After loving restoration in Seville, Our Lady of Europa once more took up her position as patroness.

With the Anglo-Dutch conquest, the statue again went into exile to avoid damage. During this time, she resided at the Chapel of Our Lady of Europe in Algeciras. Around 1864, Bishop Scandella finally negotiated the return of Our Lady of Europe to Gibraltar.

The shrine has a sibling, 'Our Lady of Africa', which is located at Ceuta, the other 'pillar of Hercules'. Prince Henry the Navigator transported this statue to its current location shortly after Portugal conquered Ceuta.

Mosque Ibrahim al Ibrahim

Gibraltar had been under the Muslim rule for over 700 years, but when the Spanish crown conquered the territory, a few radical changes were effected. King Ferdinand and Queen Isabelle were devoutly Catholic and removed nearly all signs of Islam. Some structures were Christianised such as the Cathedral of St Mary the Crowned, which had previously been a mosque, but others became casualties of this wave of cultural and religious cleansing.

Today, with Muslims making up 2000 or 4 percent of Gibraltar's overall population, the settlement once more has a mosque. The Ibrahim-al-Ibrahim Mosque is located at Europa Point and faces south towards Morocco, which is on the other side of the Strait of Gibraltar. It was a gift from King Fahd, the monarch of Saudi Arabia and was completed in 1997, after two years of construction and at a cost of £5 million. The facility includes a school, lecture hall and library. It carries two distinctions, as the largest mosque in a non-Muslim region and the southernmost mosque of Europe.

Alameda Botanic Gardens

Red Sands Road, Gibraltar

Tel: (+350) 200 72639

http://www.gibraltargardens.gi/

The Alameda Gardens was established in 1816 by General George Don, the governor of the time, to provide an area for recreation. The project was funded by public lotteries and most labor came from volunteer efforts. A section of the garden was set aside for the cultivation of much needed vegetables. The name Alameda seems to have been derived from the Spanish 'alamo' and refers to the White poplar trees that once proliferated the area.

Decorative paths and terraced areas characterize the layout, which makes extensive use of the limestone and rock features that occur naturally on Gibraltar.

Over 1600 different plant species are represented in the garden. Large portions of these are succulents, with aloe species dominating. Other notables include the stone pine, the wild olive, the European nettle tree, the Australian silk tree as well as the Canary Islands dragon tree, of which one specimen is over 300 years old. There are various assorted benches to relax.

The Gardens also has several monuments. One is dedicated to a fictitious character, Molly Bloom, who appears in Ulysses by James Joyce and was described as a native of Gibraltar. The other two are of a military nature. The Wellington monument features a bronze bust of the famous commander placed on top of a marble pillar that originally came from Roman ruins in Libya. The Elliot Memorial honors General George Augustus Eliot for his efforts in defence of Gibraltar during the Great Siege between 1779 and 1783. The grounds also feature an open-air theatre. Admission is free.

🌏 Moorish Castle Complex

Willis Road, Gibraltar

At the northern side of the Upper Rock Nature Reserve stands another marvel of Gibraltar. The original structure of the Moorish castle was completed in 1160 and represents the period of the Marinid dynasty in Morocco, but it suffered considerable damage during the first

GIBRALTAR TRAVEL GUIDE

Spanish conquest. In the 14th century, a second Moorish occupation saw the castle restored.

The complex comprises several buildings, which had separate functions. The Tower of Homage is awe-inspiring, even by modern standards. Believed to be the original castle, it can be reckoned the oldest Moorish fortification on the European continent.

Repaired upon reoccupation, it has, as a sign proclaims, withstood ten subsequent sieges.

Other parts of the complex include the inner and outer keep, which surround the Tower of Homage, and the Quasbah, which contains another of its features, namely the Gate House. Until 2010, the Complex housed

Gibraltar's prison. It is now one of the Rock's most prominent tourist attractions.

🌑 Caves of Gibraltar

Despite its modest dimensions, Gibraltar boasts around 150 caves. Some, like St Michael's Cave had been known since antiquity. Others, like Forbes Quarry, were accidental discoveries. Many of them have yielded significant prehistoric finds that can now be viewed at Gibraltar's museum.

St Michael's Cave

The largest cave on Gibraltar is a collection of limestone caves known as St Michael's Cave. Located on the Upper Rock at 300m above the sea, the caves earned an early mention by the poet Homer and the Roman geographer

Pomponius Mela. The site is associated with several mysterious legends. Since Gibraltar is believed to be one half of the Pillars of Hercules, the cave was believed to be an entrance to the realm of Hades, ruler of the underworld.

The cave has been the source of a number of interesting archaeological finds. As early as 1867, Captain Brome, in his capacity as the Governor of the military prison, uncovered various tools such as bone needles, stone axes, shell adornments and pottery. During the 1970s, a Neolithic bowl as well as cave art emerged, but the most significant find has to be two Neanderthal skulls that could date back to 40,000 years ago.

In recorded history, the caves served as a venue for Victorian parties, weddings or duels. It was used as a military hospital, as hiding place and most recently, as auditorium for concerts and other high profile events. Seating, however, is limited to 100. Admission for a guided tour is £8.00.

Gorman's Cave

Gorham's Cave on Gibraltar occupies a special place in the research into prehistoric man's activities. It is widely considered to be the last known dwelling place of the Neanderthals. While it had been previously believed that this heavy browed cousin of man died out around 35,000 years ago, the finds at Gorham's Cave tell a different story. They are believed to be only 24,000 years old.

GIBRALTAR TRAVEL GUIDE

The cave, which was discovered by Captain A. Gorham in 1907 and still bears his inscribed name, contains four separate layers of deposits that are of archaeological interest.

The most recent of these have been positively linked with the Phoenicians and date back to 300-800 BC. There are hints of a Neolithic presence in the second layer of finds, while the third level yielded Palaeolithicartefacts linked to two different cultures, the Solutrean makers of flint tools as well as the Magdalenian hunters, who crafted their weapons of bone and were fond of animal motifs. Most intriguing, though, are Mousterian tools, as these are associated with the Neanderthal people. The cave has been nominated for UNESCO World Heritage status.

Forbes Quarry

Located along the North face of Gibraltar, Forbes Quarry was mined during the 19th century to provide stone for various fortification projects. In 1848, a limestone cave was uncovered and Captain Edmund Flint discovered the skull of an adult female Neanderthal. As the find was only the second fossil of its kind to emerge, it attracted enormous attention within the scientific community. Charles Darwin specifically arranged to examine it. It was dated at between 30,000 and 50,000 years old. Unfortunately, the ongoing mining activity at Forbes Quarry somewhat compromised the possibility of further excavation at the site.

🌍 Rosia Bay

Rosia Bay faces England and is located at the southwestern tip of Gibraltar As the only natural harbour on Gibraltar, it played an important role in the Battle of Trafalgar. It was to this location that Admiral Nelson's body was brought, after his death. Today, Nelsons Anchorage serves as a museum that offers our generation great insight and background into this important victory for England. Admission is just £1.00.

On a more mundane note, the beach is suitable for bathing and fishing. With plenty of nearby watering holes, this is a great spot to relax. Nearby is the Trafalgar Cemetery.

GIBRALTAR TRAVEL GUIDE

Although set up as a place of devotion for the fallen of the Battle of Trafalgar, only two of its graves can be associated with heroes of the sea conflict. They are the occupant of graves 121 and 101, respectively the final resting place of Lieutenant William Forster and Lieutenant Thomas Norman. Other graves represent casualties of conflicts such as the battles of Algeciras, Cadiz and Malaga and also victims of other hostilities from the Napoleonic Wars.

Rosia Bay is guarded by Parson's Lodge, an important battery which is well positioned for anyone wishing to hold the Rock, as the British have done for several centuries.

🌎 Gibraltar Museum

Off Main Street, Gibraltar

http://www.gibmuseum.gi/

The museum of Gibraltar is home to a wide variety of artefacts representing different and vastly divergent eras. Its most famous exhibits have to be the prehistoric finds the Rock's caves have yielded to excavators. While some represent more recent settlements, the ones of particular significance have to do with the region's Neanderthal presence.

The Egyptian mummy of Gibraltar dates back to 800BCE, and it originated from a shipwreck in the area in 1930. In the basement, you can admire the remains of the Moorish baths, with its impressive hydraulic and ventilation systems. Another interesting display is the incredibly detailed scale model of the entire Rock of Gibraltar, as painstakingly created by Lieutenant Charles Warren around 1865.

The museum opened in 1930 and regularly hosts lectures, particularly on evolution. Its present director, Clive Finlayson is a native of Gibraltar. He had worked on various excavation sites around the region and has authored several books on Gibraltar's prehistoric heritage. Admission to the museum is £2.50.

🌍 Casemates Square

Casemates Square is located at one end of Main Street. It is the scene of outdoor restaurants, shops and food vendors, where you can expect buskers and cther street entertainers during the holiday season. Here you will find the Tourist Information Center.

The Moors first fortified the area, which had once been the beachfront. It still remains somewhat sandy. The Spanish added a water gate and transformed it into a shipyard. During the 1990s, the remains of an old galley house from this era were uncovered.

The British added battlements and solidified the general foundations of the square, which had become waterlogged and unstable. After the Great Siege of 1779-1783, several buildings were destroyed and the wide-open plaza became the setting for military parades, but also public executions, a practice that only ended in the mid-1860s. The Ceremony of the Keys, a military parade that mimics a similarly named event at the Tower of London, takes place on Casemates Square every evening. This tradition survives from the 1700s.

John Mackintosh Square

Also known as the Piazza, John Mackintosh Square had been the main plaza of Gibraltar's settled areas in Spanish times.

It had been called Plaza Mayor, Commercial Square, Plazuela del Martillo and the Piazza, until the name John Mackintosh Square was finally adopted in 1940. John Mackintosh was born on Gibraltar and had made his fortune selling coal to the Navy. Throughout his life and also in the bequest of his will, he applied his means to the help the poor and the needy, particularly on Gibraltar.

During the 1500s, the square had boasted a fountain, although this later fell into disrepair. During the early part of British occupation, it was used for military parades and also for public floggings. The square is flanked by the City Hall, which had originally been the mansion of Aaron Cardozo, a wealthy Jewish merchant.

🌐 100 Ton Gun

The 100-ton gun of Gibraltar is mounted at the Napier of Magdala Battery, a feat of Victorian engineering. It was part of a greater project of coastal defence of the time, involving the bases of Gibraltar and Malta. Twelve guns were originally built by Sir W. C. Armstrong at Newcastle-Upon-Tyne, of which eight had been commissioned by the

Italian Navy. Of the remaining four, two were sent to Gibraltar and the other two to Malta.

The gun's dimensions are quite impressive. The length of the barrel is 9.95 m and it has the capacity of firing on a target up to 12.8km away. Its muzzle velocity is 469.39m per second, and it can be fired every four minutes. Gun enthusiasts would definitely be awed at the sight of this relic from a bygone era. The only other gun of its kind still in use is the one at Fort Rinella in Malta.

Churches of Gibraltar

Gibraltar has two cathedrals, but when people speak of The Cathedral, they are usually referring to the older, Catholic one, the Cathedral of St Mary the Crowned. From the 14th century, a mosque stood on the site, but when the Christian forces of Spain recaptured the territory in 1462, it was decreed that the location should be Christianised. The courtyard is still reminiscent of Moorish origins, but the Church itself is Gothic in style.

The Cathedral of the Holy Trinity was completed in 1832, but only achieved official status as a Cathedral of the Anglican Church in 1842, with the appointment of George Tomlinson as its first bishop.

The Church of Scotland in Gibraltar is represented by St Andrew's Church, which was completed early in 1854. Constructed of limestone and featuring beautiful stained glass windows, it provided a place of worship for the growing number of Scottish soldiers stationed at Gibraltar. Interestingly, the Church enjoys close ties with another

Presbyterian congregation in Costa del Sol. Gibraltar is a popular marriage destination, but St Andrew's, unlike some of the other churches on the Rock, also caters for previously divorced couples.

Budget Tips

 # Accommodation

Con Dios

Marina Bay, Gibraltar 11300

On Gibraltar, space is limited. Therefore some very

interesting accommodation solutions are sometimes found.

Con Dios is a boat located within the marina of Gibraltar that doubles as a bed and breakfast establishment. Bathroom facilities are shared and some of the cabins are larger than others. The port and the starboard rooms are quite small. While some facilities such as air-conditioning can be problematic, the owners of the yacht are described as super helpful in all respects. There are facilities for making coffee and tea, a DVD player and free Wifi access. The sun deck is a great place to relax. Accommodation begins at £25.

Bristol Hotel

8/10 Cathedral Square, Gibraltar

Conveniently located just five minutes away from the cable car to the Upper Rock Nature Reserve, the Bristol Hotel is well equipped to ensure a pleasant and comfortable stay. Rooms at the Bristol Hotel include bathroom and shower facilities, television, a fridge, air-conditioning and plenty of storage space. The hotel includes a swimming pool. Wifi access is available in the lounge. Accommodation begins at £55 a night and a buffet breakfast is included.

Queen's Hotel

1 Boyd St, Gibraltar

Tel: (+350) 200 74000

http://www.queenshotel.gi/

Hotel accommodation tends to be quite pricey in Gibraltar,

but at the Queen's Hotel you can expect to see your basic needs met at affordable prices. All rooms include satellite television, en-suite bathroom facilities, air-conditioning and free Wifi Internet access. The hotel is located close to the cable car as well as the Alameda Botanical Gardens. Accommodation begins at £60 a night and includes breakfast.

Cannon Hotel

9 Cannon Lane, Gibraltar

http://www.cannonhotel.gi/

The Cannon Hotel is a family hotel of modest proportions, located just off Main Road near the Cathedral. The staff is described as friendly and helpful, but beware, the street-side rooms can be noisy. There is a bar in the courtyard.

Bathroom facilities are communal. Free Wifi coverage is included. Accommodation begins at £42.00 and includes a full English breakfast.

Governor's Inn

36 Governor's Street, Gibraltar

Tel: (+350) 200 44227

The self-catering apartments at the Governor's Inn are comfortable and well maintained, combining independent living with the creature comforts of a home away from home. The kitchen includes a fridge, microwave, kettle, toaster, crockery, cutlery and cookware. You will also find a washing machine, cable TV, a DVD player and a safe. The apartments are located near Main Street, Casemates Square and John Mackintosh Square. Accommodation is

£65 per apartment, meaning that several people sharing can cut their costs significantly.

Places to Eat

Gatsby's

1 - 3 Watergardens 1, Waterport Ave, Gibraltar

Tel: (+350) 200 76291

http://www.gatsbys.gi/

The menu at Gatsby's is based on a medley of English, French, Spanish and Indian cuisine. Included among the mains, which cost between £12.95 and £17.95, are items such as Chicken Blue Cheese, Scallopini Marsala, Char Grilled Beef Tenderloin and Honey & Soy Glazed Salmon.

The starters feature items such as the Lamb Sheesh Kebabs at £6.95, Tiger Prawns Pil Pil and Chicken Samosas. The house salad contains the interesting mix of goat's cheese, walnuts, pine nuts and sultanas. Service is described as friendly and attentive.

Bean & Gone Cafe

20 Engineers Lane, Gibraltar 00000

Tel: (+350) 200 65334

http://www.beanandgonecafe.com/

At Bean & Gone Cafe, you can expect to enjoy good coffee and great homemade food. Vegetarians would be pleased to discover that there is an extensive selection of vegan and vegetarian items such as Tabbouleh, which is a couscous dish, lentil salad, grape & walnut salad as well as a few vegetarian pasta options. Under light meals, you will find paninis, wraps and baguettes, which are freshly baked every day and cost no more than £3.50, as well as several burger combinations at around £5.50. A choice of breakfasts is served, costing £5.50 or under. Bean & Gone Cafe will deliver bulk orders if necessary.

Sacarello's Gibraltar

57 Irish Town, Gibraltar

Tel: (+350) 200 70625

http://www.sacarellosgibraltar.com/

The coffee shop/restaurant Sacarello's is located within the section of Gibraltar known as Irish Town, since it once housed the Irish quarter of the military barracks. The menu features a variety of meals ranging from light to main. Among the sandwiches, you will find the Smoked Salmon sandwich, costing £6.80, cheese and ham for £3.80 and cream cheese and cucumber for £3.90. Main meals include Spaghetti Bolognaise for £7.80, Tagliatelle Carbonara for £8.10, Lasagne for £8.50 and Fillet Steak for £15.25. The bakery offers lighter treats such as scones, cheesecake, apple pie, gateaux and sundaes. There is also a selection of coffees and speciality teas on the menu.

Bianca's

6/7 Admiral's Walk, Marina Bay, Gibraltar

Tel: (+350) 200 73379

http://www.biancas.gi/

As a well-established cafe located at Gibraltar's attractive marina development, Bianca's is popular with locals and visitors alike.

The menu boasts a great choice in meals. The pizza, priced between £7.25 and £9.45 includes favorites such as tropical, four seasons and napolitana, as well some more unusual combinations such as the "hot" colonels, which features as toppings chicken, sweet corn, mango, jalapenos and chutney. Main meals include tender roasted lamb shank for £14.25, chicken and drunken prawns which features chicken breast cooked in a sweet, coconut cream sauce with prawns for £10.45, Thai chicken and vegetable curry for £10.95, fillet, spare ribs, pork loin and even cheese and bacon burgers. The menu includes an interesting selection of cocktails and desserts. Breakfast is also served. Some of Bianca's more celebrated dinner guests include HRH Prince Andrew,

Carlos Santana, Jane Russell and the singer-songwriter Albert Hammond, who is a native of Gibraltar.

Cafe Solo

Grand Casemates Square 3, Town Centre, Gibraltar

Tel: (+350) 200 44449

Located on Grand Casemates Square, Cafe Solo offers Italian cuisine such as pizza, pasta and salads as well as a lively atmosphere. Among the light meals and pastries you will find pannini and toasted sandwiches, priced at £3.25 and under, as well as muffins, bagels, croissants and Danish.

Pasta options include penne, tagliatelle and linguine. Salads range from standard combinations such as Greek to the more inventive Goat's cheese salad. Lamb Tagine spices up a lamb shank to serve it North African style with couscous and crusty bread for £14.75. Do inquire about the daily specials, as they are subject to change.

🌎 Shopping

Thanks to the duty free status of its shops, Gibraltar is a popular location to shop and save a little money as many of its prices compare favourably with nearby towns and cities. It is particularly advantageous to stock up on alcohol and cigarettes while on the Rock. You can also expect bargains in perfumes or electronic goods.

Duty-Free Shopping

Lewis Stagnetto Ltd is well established at 41 Main Street (Tel: 350 200 43274) and specializes in Cuban cigars across a variety of price ranges. Anglo Hispano at 5-7 Main Street has been wine wholesaler for more than a hundred years. The Duty Free Shop at Gibraltar's airport is another stop for great savings. Do remember the limits. You will be allowed 200 cigarettes or 50 cigars, 2 litres of wine, 1 litre of spirits and 60 ml of perfume.

Buying Jewellery

A great place for buying jewellery at reduced prices is Gibrocks, which occupies 295 Main Street. They stock a good range of gold, diamonds and other precious stones. The Silver Shop can be found at 9-13 Horse Barrack Lane. Here you can buy a variety of silver crafted jewellery.

Gibraltar Crystal Factory

Grand Casemates Square

Tel: (+350) 200 50136

Visit the factory to watch a demonstration of the art of glass blowing and then check out the exhibited goods. Glass and crystal ornaments can be bought in a wide variety of colors ranging from cobalt blue, Mediterranean blue, amber, cranberry, amethyst and the multicolored Harlequin combination.

If you have an artistic flair, you could even try to design your own wine glasses. Gibraltar Crystal also handles engraving and produces unique designer paperweights. Expect to be delighted by the wide selection, even if you go only to browse. The retail outlet is located near the factory.

Electronics

One highly recommended shop is Galaxy at 175 Main Street. Staff members are very informative and offer good prices and advice on stock such as cameras, memory cards and DVD players. The PC Clinic at 15-17 Convent Place (Tel: +350 200-4-999-1) sells and repairs electronic goods. They stock PCs, laptops, netbooks, hardware, software, peripherals and accessories.

Main Street, Gibraltar

The chief shopping region of Gibraltar can be found along Main Street. Here you will find outlets of various international brands such as La Senza, Accessorize,

Tommy

Hilfiger, Next, The Body Shop and also the British favorite

Marks & Spencer

Know Before You Go

Entry Requirements

By virtue of the Schengen agreement, visitors from other countries in the European Union will not need a visa when visiting Spain. Additionally visitors from Switzerland, Norway, Lichtenstein, Iceland, Canada, the United Kingdom, Australia and the USA are also exempt. Independently travelling minors will need to carry written permission from their parents. If visiting from a country where you require a visa to enter Spain, you will also need to state the purpose of your visit and provide proof that you have financial means to support yourself for the duration of your stay. Unless you are an EU national, your passport should be valid for at least 3 months after the end of your stay.

Health Insurance

Citizens of other EU countries are covered for emergency health care in Spain. UK residents, as well as visitors from Switzerland are covered by the European Health Insurance Card (EHIC), which can be applied for free of charge. Visitors from non-Schengen countries will need to show proof of private health insurance that is valid for the duration of their stay in Spain, as part of their visa application.

🌐 Travelling with Pets

Spain participates in the Pet Travel Scheme (PETS) which allows UK residents to travel with their pets without requiring quarantine upon re-entry. Certain conditions will need to be met. The animal will have to be microchipped and up to date on rabies vaccinations. Additionally, you will need a PETS re-entry certificate issued by a UK vet, an Export Health Certificate (this is required by the Spanish authorities), an official Certificate of Treatment against dangerous parasites such as tapeworm and ticks and an official Declaration that your pet has not left the qualifying countries within this period. Pets from the USA or Canada may be brought in under the conditions of a non-commercial import. For this, your pet will also need to be microchipped (or marked with an identifying tattoo) and up to date on rabies vaccinations.

🌐 Airports

Adolfo Suárez Madrid–Barajas Airport (MAD) is the largest and busiest airport in Spain. It is located about 9km from the financial district of Madrid, the capital. The busiest route is the so-called "Puente Aéreo" or "air bridge", which connects Madrid with Barcelona. The second busiest airport in Spain is **Barcelona–El Prat Airport** (BCN), located about 14km southwest from the center of Barcelona. There are two terminals. The newer Terminal 1 handles the bulk of its traffic, while the older Terminal 2 is used by budget airlines such as EasyJet.

Palma de Mallorca Airport (PMI) is the third largest airport in Spain and one of its busiest in the summer time. It has the capacity of processing 25 million passengers annually. **Gran Canaria Airport** (LPA) handles around 10 million passengers annually and connects travellers with the Canary Islands. **Pablo Ruiz Picasso Malaga Airport** (AGP) provides access to the Costa del Sol. Other southern airports are **Seville Airport** (SVQ), **Jaen Federico Garcia Lorca Airport** (GRX) near Granada, **Jerez de la Frontera Airport**, which connects travellers to Costa del Luz and Cadiz and **Almeria Airport** (LEI).

🌍 Airlines

Iberia is the flag carrying national airline of Spain. Since a merger in 2010 with British Airways, it is part of the International Airlines Group (IAG). Iberia is in partnership with the regional carrier Air Nostrum and Iberia Express, which focusses on medium and short haul routes. Vueling is a low-cost Spanish airline with connections to over 100 destinations. In partnership with MTV, it also provides a seasonal connection to Ibiza. Volotea is a budget airline based in Barcelona, which mainly flies to European destinations. Air Europe, the third largest airline after Iberia and Vueling connects Europe to resorts in the Canaries and the Balearic Islands and also flies to North and South America. Swiftair flies mainly to destinations in Europe, North Africa and the Middle East.

Barcelona-El Prat Airport serves as a primary hub for Iberia Regional. It is also a hub for Vueling. Additionally it functions as a regional hub for Ryanair. Air Europe's primary hubs are at Palma de Mallorca Airport and Madrid Barajas Airport, but other bases are at Barcelona Airport and Tenerife South Airport. Air Nostrum is served by hubs at Barcelona Airport, Madrid Barajas Airport and Valencia Airport. Gran Canaria Airport is the hub for the regional airline, Binter Canarias.

🌏 Currency

Spain's currency is the Euro. It is issued in notes in denominations of €500, €200, €100, €50, €20, €10 and €5. Coins are issued in denominations of €2, €1, 50c, 20c, 10c, 5c, 2c and 1c.

🌐 Banking & ATMs

You should have no trouble making withdrawals in Spain if your ATM card is compatible with the MasterCard/Cirrus or Visa/Plus networks. If you want to save money, avoid using the dynamic currency conversion (DCC) system, which promises to charge you in your own currency for the Euros you withdraw. The fine print is that your rate will be less favorable. Whenever possible, opt to conduct your transaction in Euros instead. Do remember to advise your bank or credit card company of your travel plans before leaving.

🌐 Credit Cards

Visa and MasterCard will be accepted at most outlets that handle credit cards in Spain, but you may find that your American Express card is not as welcome at all establishments. While shops may still be able to accept transactions with older magnetic strip cards, you will need a PIN enabled card for transactions at automatic vendors such as ticket sellers. Do not be offended when asked to show proof of ID when paying by credit card. It is common practice in Spain and Spaniards are required by law to carry identification on them at all times.

🌏 Tourist Taxes

In the region of Catalonia, which includes Barcelona, a tourist tax of between €0.45 and €2.50 per night is levied for the first seven days of your stay. The amount depends on the standard of the establishment, but includes youth hostels, campgrounds, holiday apartments and cruise ships with a stay that exceeds 12 hours.

🌏 Reclaiming VAT

If you are not from the European Union, you can claim back VAT (or Value Added Tax) paid on your purchases in Spain. The VAT rate in Spain is 18 percent. VAT refunds are made on purchases of €90.15 and over from a single shop. Look for shops displaying Global Blue Tax Free Shopping signage. You will be required to fill in a form at the shop, which must then be stamped at the Customs office at the airport. Customs officers will want to inspect your purchases to make sure that they are sealed and unused. Once this is done, you will be able to claim your refund from the Refund Office at the airport. Alternately, you can mail the form to Global Blue once you get home for a refund on your credit card.

🌍 Tipping policy

In general, Spain does not really have much of a tipping culture and the Spanish are not huge tippers themselves. When in a restaurant, check your bill to see whether a gratuity is already included. If not, the acceptable amount will depend on the size of the meal, the prestige of the restaurant and the time of day. For a quick coffee, you can simply round the amount off. For lunch in a modest establishment, opt for 5 percent or one euro per person. The recommended tip for dinner would be more generous, usually somewhere between 7 and 10 percent. This will depend on the type of establishment.

In hotels, if there is someone to help you with your luggage, a tip of 1 euro should be sufficient. At railway stations and airports, a tip is not really expected. Rounding off the amount of the fare to the nearest euro would be sufficient for a taxi driver. If you recruited a private driver, you may wish to tip that person at the end of your association with him.

🌍 Mobile Phones

Most EU countries, including Spain uses the GSM mobile service. This means that most UK phones and some US and Canadian phones and mobile devices will work in Spain. While you could check with your service provider about coverage before you leave, using your own service in roaming mode will involve additional costs. The alternative is to purchase a Spanish SIM card to use during your stay in Spain.

Spain has four mobile networks. They are Movistar, Vodafone, Orange and Yoiga. Buying a Spanish SIM card is relatively simple and inexpensive. By law, you will be required to show some form of identification such as a passport. A basic SIM card from Vodafone costs €5. There are two tourist packages available for €15, which offers a combination of 1Gb data, together with local and international call time. Alternately, a data only package can also be bought for €15. From Orange, you can get a SIM card for free, with a minimum top-up purchase of €10. A tourist SIM with a combination of data and voice calls can be bought for €15. Movistar offers a start-up deal of €10. At their sub-branches, Tuenti, you can also get a free SIM, but the catch is that you need to choose a package to get it. The start-up cost at Yoiga is €20.

☺ Dialling Code

The international dialling code for Spain is +34.

🌐 Emergency Numbers

All Emergencies: 112 (no area code required)

Police (municipal): 092

Police (national): 091

Police (tourist police, Madrid): 91 548 85 37

Police (tourist police, Barcelona): 93 290 33 27

Ambulance: 061 or 112

Fire: 080 or 112

Traffic: 900 123 505

Electricity: 900 248 248

Immigration: 900 150 000

MasterCard: 900 958 973

Visa: 900 99 1124

🌐 Public Holidays

1 January: New Year's Day (Año Nuevo)

6 January: Day of the Epiphany/Three Kings Day (Reyes Mago)

March/April: Good Friday

1 May: Labor Day (Día del Trabajo)

15 August: Assumption of Mary (Asunción de la Virgen)

12 October: National Day of Spain/Columbus Day (Fiesta Nacional de España or Día de la Hispanidad)

1 November: All Saints Day (Fiesta de Todos los Santos)

6 December: Spanish Constitution Day (Día de la Constitución)

8 December: Immaculate Conception (La Immaculada)

25 December: Christmas (Navidad)

Easter Monday is celebrated in the Basque region, Castile-La Mancha, Catalonia, La Rioja, Navarra and Valencia. 26 December is celebrated as Saint Stephen's Day in Catalonia and the Balearic Islands.

🌐 Time Zone

Spain falls in the Central European Time Zone. This can be calculated as Greenwich Mean Time/Co-ordinated Universal Time (GMT/UTC) +2; Eastern Standard Time (North America) -6; Pacific Standard Time (North America) -9.

🌐 Daylight Savings Time

Clocks are set forward one hour on the last Sunday in March and set back one hour on the last Sunday in October for Daylight Savings Time.

🌎 School Holidays

Spain's academic year is from mid-September to mid-June. It is divided into three terms with two short breaks of about two weeks around Christmas and Easter.

🌎 Trading Hours

Trading hours in Spain usually run from 9.30am to 1.30pm and from 4.30pm to 8pm, from Mondays to Saturdays. Malls and shopping centers often trade from 10am to 9pm without closing. During the peak holiday seasons, shops could stay open until 10pm. Lunch is usually served between 1pm and 3.30pm while dinner is served from 8.30 to 11pm.

🌎 Driving Laws

The Spanish drive on the right hand side of the road. You will need a driver's licence which is valid in the EC to be able to hire a car in Spain. The legal driving age is 18, but most rental companies will require you to be at least 21 to be able to rent a car. You will need to carry your insurance documentation and rental contract with you at all times, when driving. The speed limit in Spain is 120km per hour on motorways, 100km per hour on dual carriageways and 90km per hour on single carriageways. Bear in mind that it is illegal to drive in Spain wearing sandals or flip-flops.

You may drive a non-Spanish vehicle in Spain provided that it is considered roadworthy in the country where it is registered. As a UK resident, you will be able to drive a vehicle registered in the UK in Spain for up to six months, provided that your liabilities as a UK motorist, such as MOT, road tax and insurance are up to date for the entire period of your stay. The legal limit in Spain is 0.05, but for new drivers who have had their licence for less than two years, it is 0.03.

Drinking Laws

In Spain, the minimum drinking age is 18. Drinking in public places is forbidden and can be punished with a spot fine. In areas where binge drinking can be a problem, alcohol trading hours are often limited.

Smoking Laws

In the beginning of 2006, Spain implemented a policy banning smoking from all public and private work places. This includes schools, libraries, museums, stadiums, hospitals, cinemas, theatres and shopping centers as well as public transport. From 2011, smoking was also banned in restaurants and bars, although designated smoking areas can be created provided they are enclosed and well ventilated. Additionally tobacco products may only be sold from tobacconists and bars and restaurants where smoking is permitted. Smoking near children's parks, schools or health centers carries a €600 fine.

🌐 Electricity

Electricity: 220 volts

Frequency: 50 Hz

Your electrical appliances from the UK and Ireland should be able to function sufficiently in Spain, but since Spain uses 2 pin sockets, you will need a C/F adapter to convert the plug from 3 to 2-pins. The voltage and frequency is compatible with UK appliances. If travelling from the USA, you will need a converter or step-down transformer to convert your appliances to 110 volts. The latest models of many laptops, camcorders, cell phones and digital cameras are dual-voltage with a built in converter.

🌐 Food & Drink

Spanish cuisine is heavily influenced by a Moorish past. Staple dishes include the rice dish, Paella, Jamon Serrano (or Spanish ham), Gazpacho (cold tomato-based vegetable soup), roast suckling pig, chorizo (spicy sausage) and the Spanish omelette. Tapas (hot or cold snacks) are served with drinks in Spanish bars.

The most quintessentially Spanish drink is sangria, but a popular alternative with the locals is tinto de verano, or summer wine, a mix of red wine and lemonade. Vino Tinto or red wine compliments most meal choices. The preferred red grape type is Tempranillo, for which the regions of Roija and Ribera del Duero are famous. A well-known sparkling wine, Cava, is grown in Catalonia. Do try the Rebujito, a Seville style mix of sherry, sparkling water and mint. The most popular local beers are Cruzcampo, Alhambra and Estrello Damm. Coffee is also popular with Spaniards, who prefer Café con leche (espresso with milk).

Websites

http://www.idealspain.com

A detailed resource that includes legal information for anyone planning a longer stay or residency in Spain.

http://spainattractions.es/

http://www.tourspain.org/

http://spainguides.com/

http://www.travelinginspain.com/

http://wikitravel.org/en/Spain

Printed in Great Britain
by Amazon